CONTEMPORARY CHRISTIAN WEDDING SONGS

FINGER GUITAR STYLE NOTES & TAB

ARRANGED BY MARCEL ROBINSON

ISBN 0-634-02975-4

HAL•LEONARD®
CORPORATION

7777 W. BLUEMOUND RD. P.O. BOX 13819 MILWAUKEE, WI 53213

Visit Hal Leonard Online at
www.halleonard.com

Cherish the Treasure

Words and Music by John Mohr

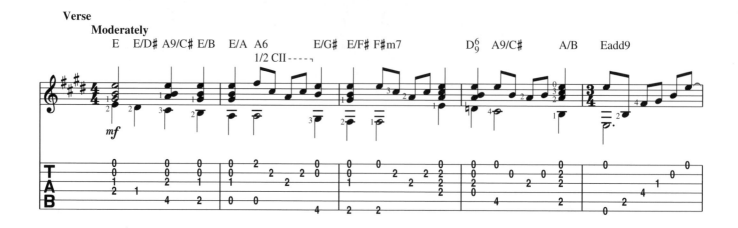

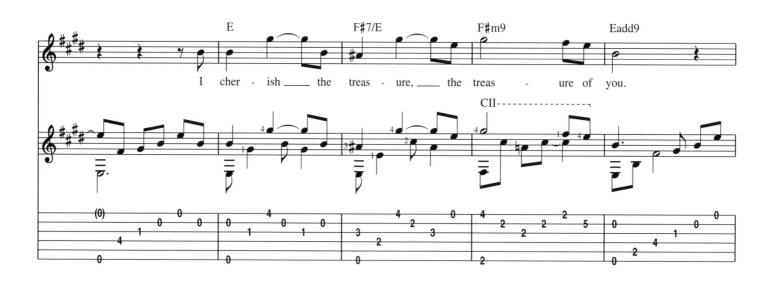

God Causes All Things to Grow

Words and Music by Steven Curtis Chapman and Steve Green

Drop D tuning:
(low to high) D–A–D–G–B–E

Intro
Moderately slow

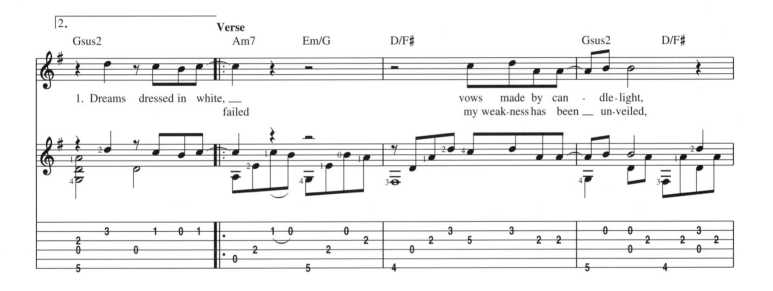

1. Dreams dressed in white, ___ failed
vows made by can - dle-light,
my weak-ness has been ___ un-veiled,

hop-ing to find ___ out what ___ true love is all ___ a - bout.
and yet, by grace ___ You choose ___ to love and to ___ for - give. ___

Interlude

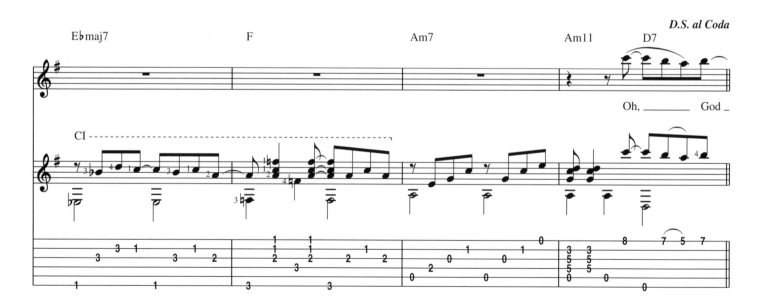

D.S. al Coda

Coda

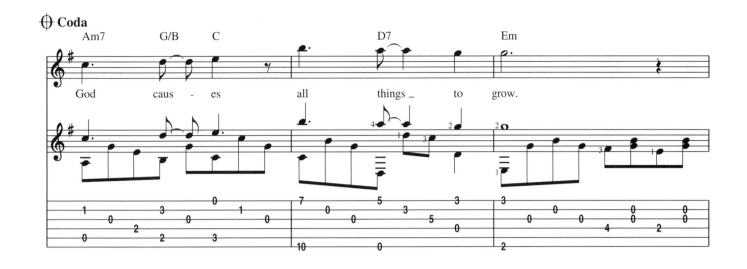

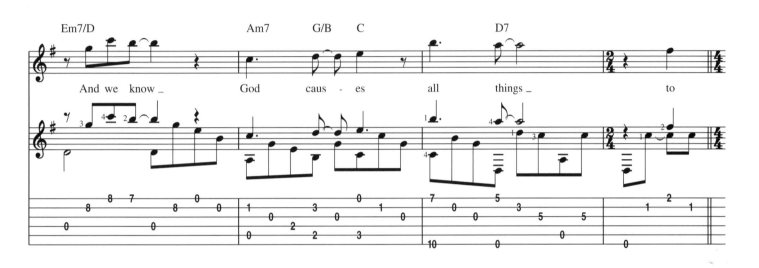

Outro

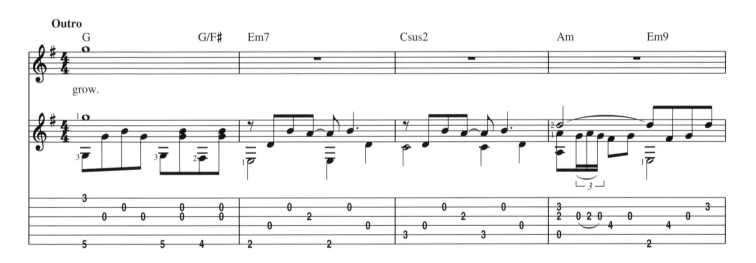

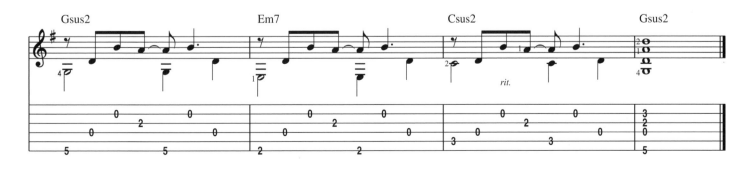

Commitment Song

Words and Music by Robert Sterling and Chris Machen

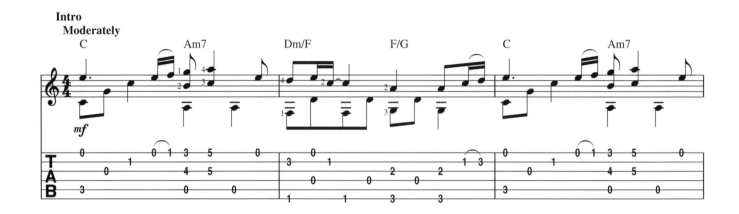

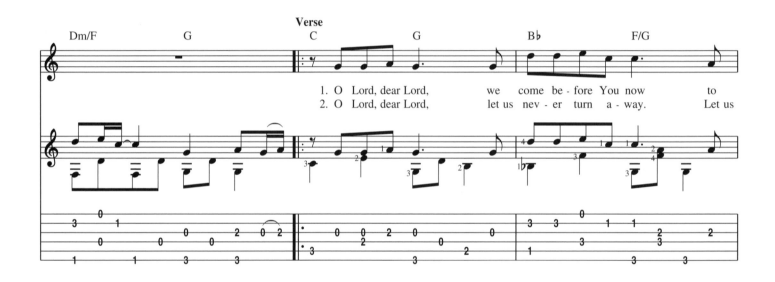

1. O Lord, dear Lord, we come be - fore You now to
2. O Lord, dear Lord, let us nev - er turn a - way. Let us

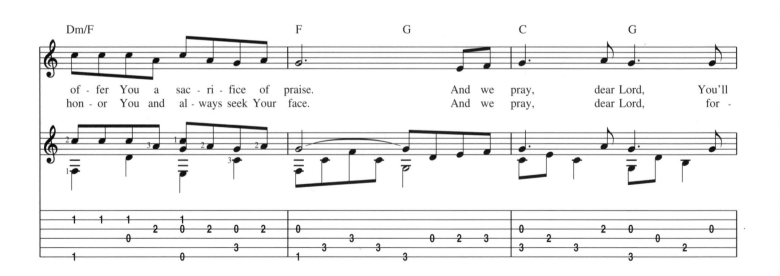

of - fer You a sac - ri - fice of praise. And we pray, dear Lord, You'll
hon - or You and al - ways seek Your face. And we pray, dear Lord, for -

bless our sol - emn vow that as long as we're to - geth - er _____ the name of Je - sus will be

give us when we stray; lead us back with ten - der mer - cy _____ with Your pre - cious love and

Chorus

raised. _____

grace. _____

O _____ Lord, dear Lord, we praise Your ho - ly name. We're

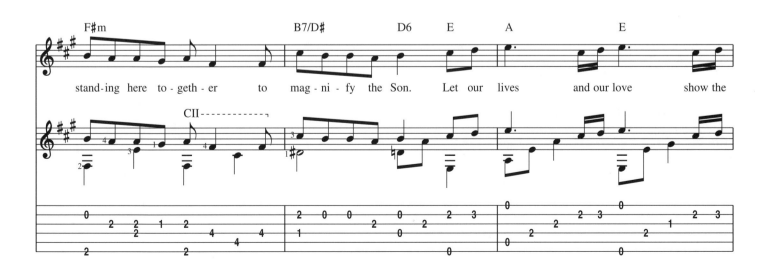

stand - ing here to - geth - er to mag - ni - fy the Son. Let our lives and our love show the

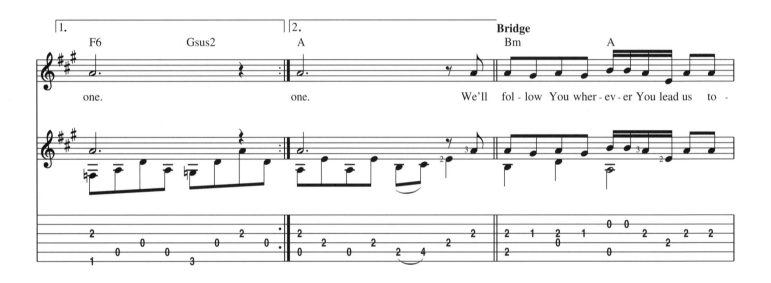

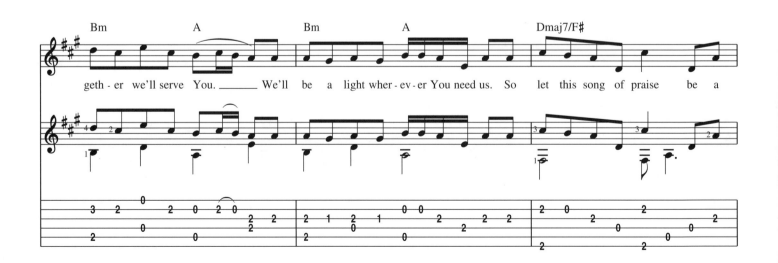

Go There With You

Words and Music by Steven Curtis Chapman

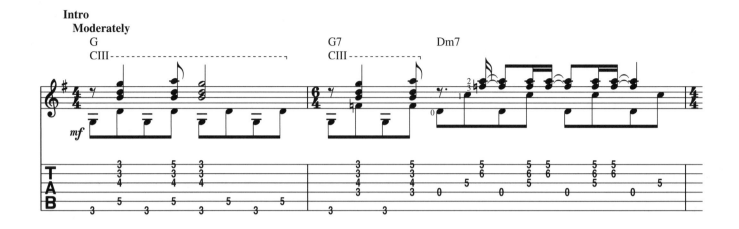

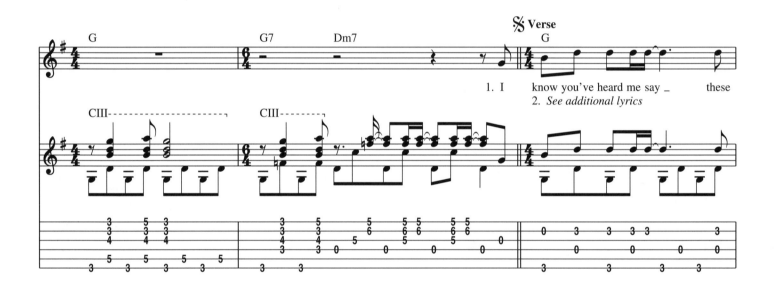

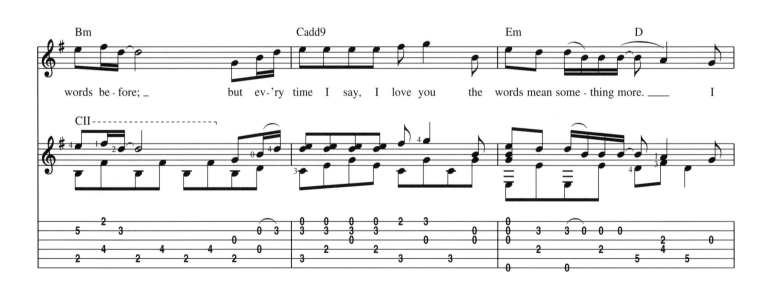

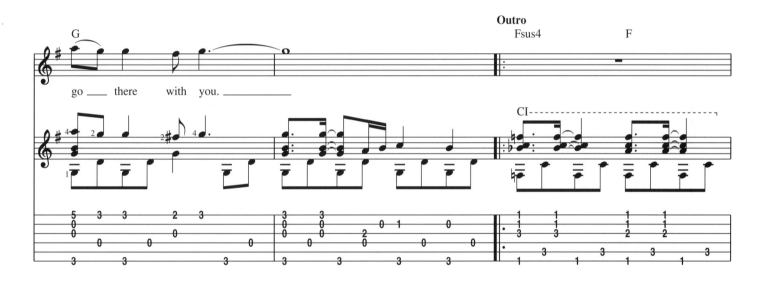

Additional Lyrics

2. I see it in your tears, you wonder where you are.
   The wind is growing colder and the sky is growing dark.
   Though it's something neither of us understands,
   We can walk through this together if we hold each other's hand.
   I said for better or for worse, I'd be with you;
   So no matter where you're going, I will go there, too.

Household of Faith

Words by Brent Lamb
Music by John Rosasco

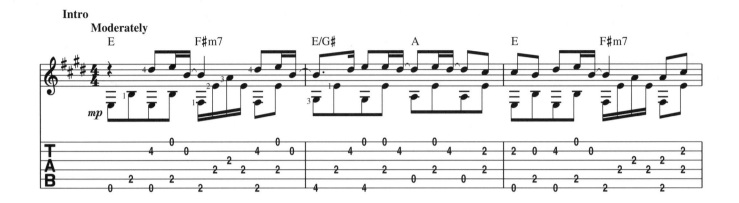

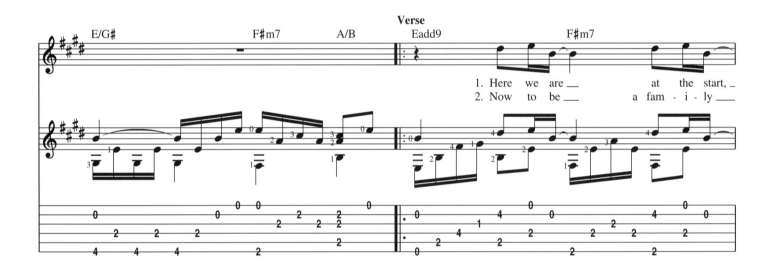

1. Here we are ___ at the start, ___
2. Now to be ___ a fam - i - ly ___

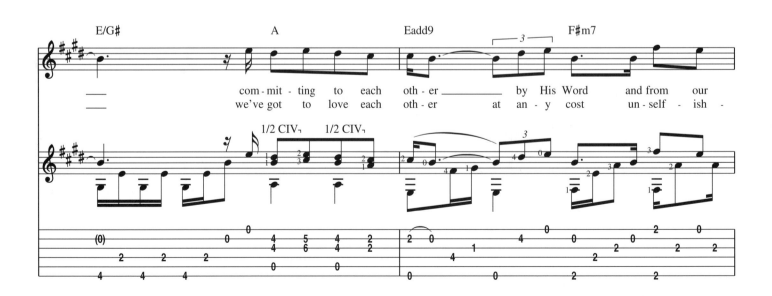

com - mit - ting to each oth - er ___ by His Word and from our
we've got to love each oth - er at an - y cost un - self - ish -

I Will Be Here

Words and Music by Steven Curtis Chapman

Drop D tuning:
(low to high) D–A–D–G–B–E

How Beautiful

Words and Music by Twila Paris

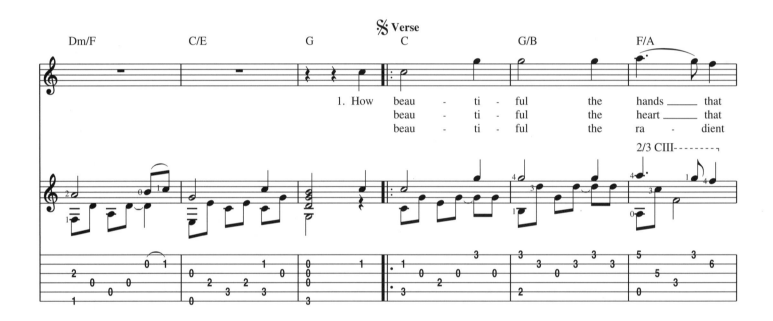

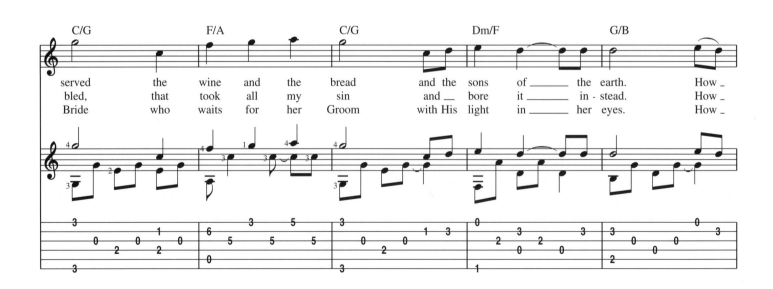

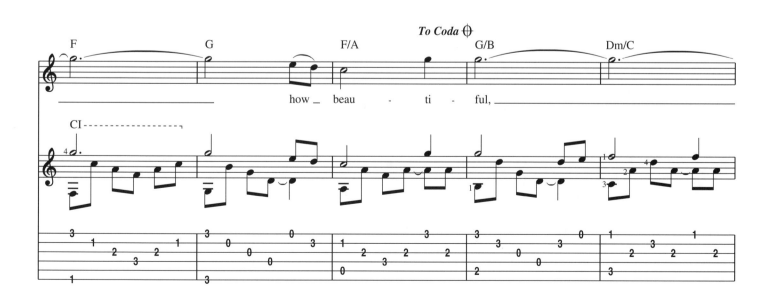

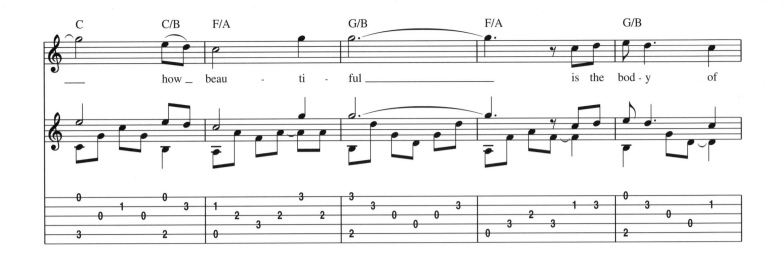

how _ beau - ti - ful _____ is the bod - y of

Christk. _____ 2. How Christ.

Bridge

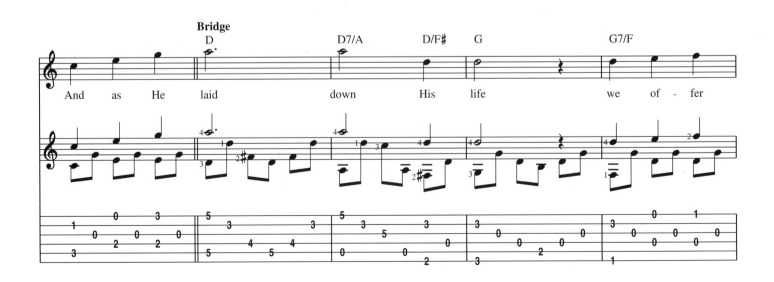

And as He laid down His life we of - fer

this — sac - ri - fice — that we will __ live

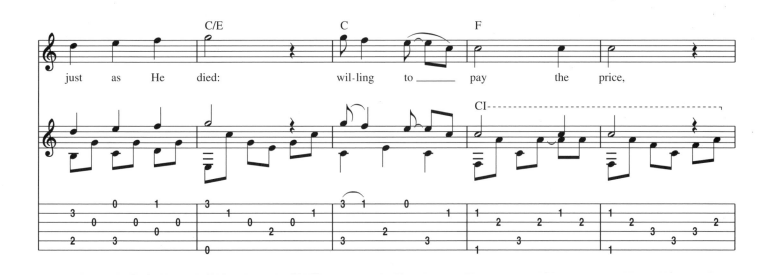

just as He died: — wil-ling to _____ pay the price,

D.S. al Coda

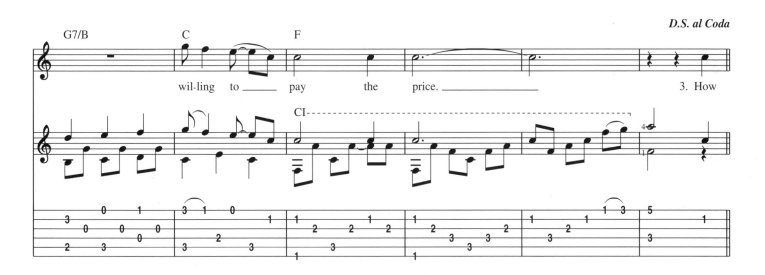

wil-ling to _____ pay the price. _____ 3. How

Coda

ful _____ is the Bod-y of Christ. _____

Outro-Verse

_____ How beau - ti - ful the feet that

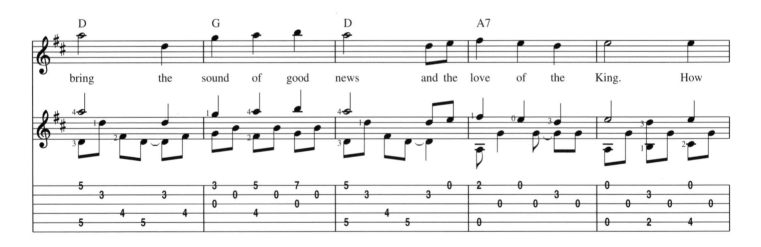

bring the sound of good news and the love of the King. How

beau - ti - ful the hands that serve the wine and the

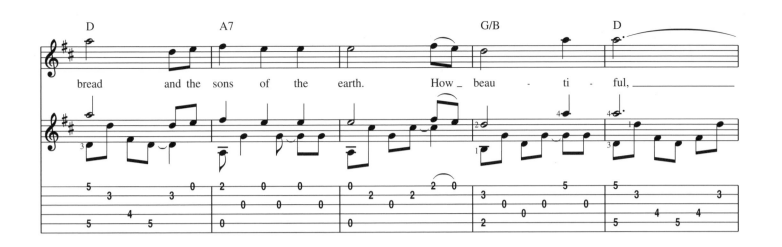

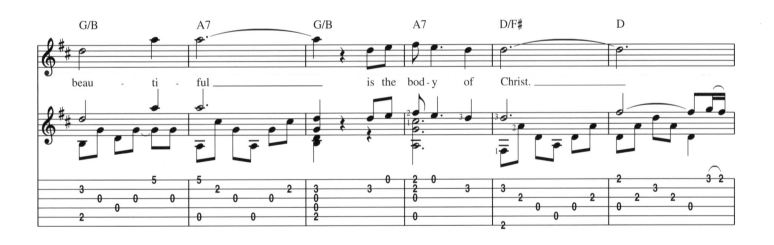

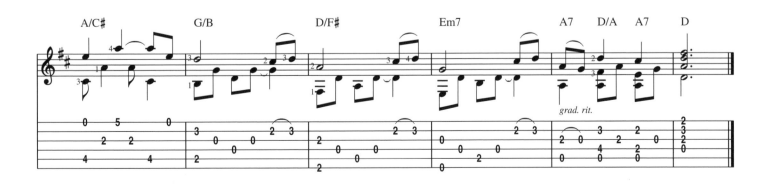

The Language of Jesus Is Love

Words and Music by Phill McHugh, Greg Nelson, Scott Wesley Brown and Phil Naish

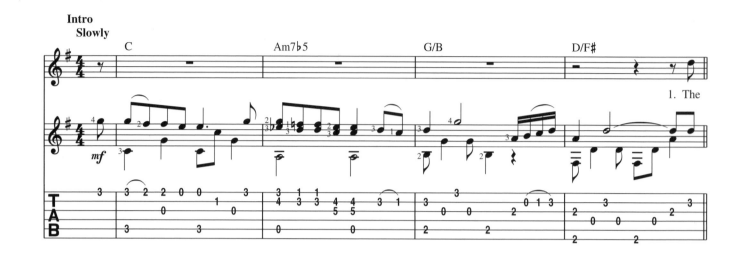

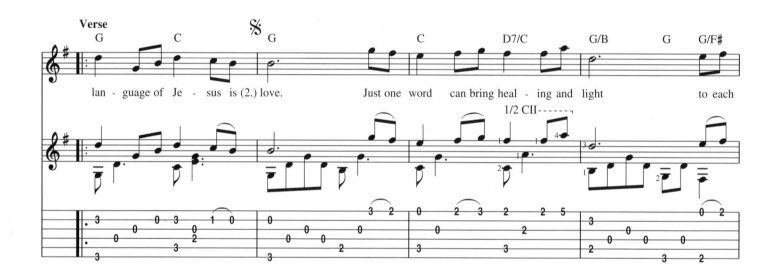

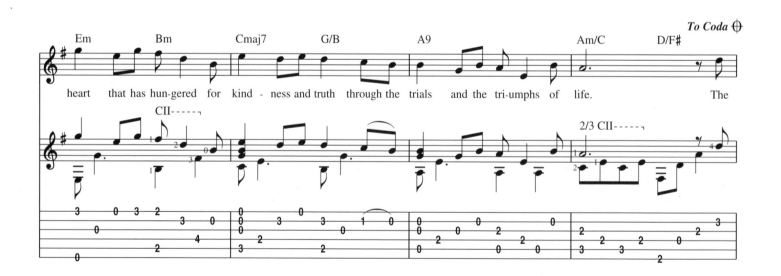

D.S. al Coda

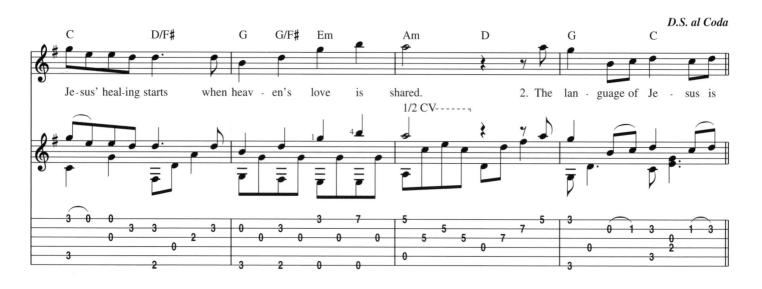

lan - guage of Je - sus is love. _____

_____ The lan - guage of Je - sus is love. _____

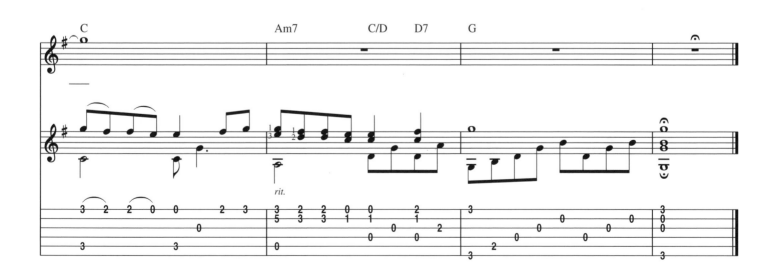

Love Will Be Our Home

Words and Music by Steven Curtis Chapman

Drop D tuning:
(low to high) D–A–D–G–B–E

Intro
Moderately

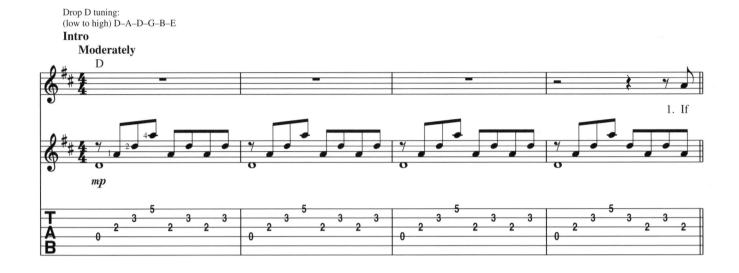

Verse

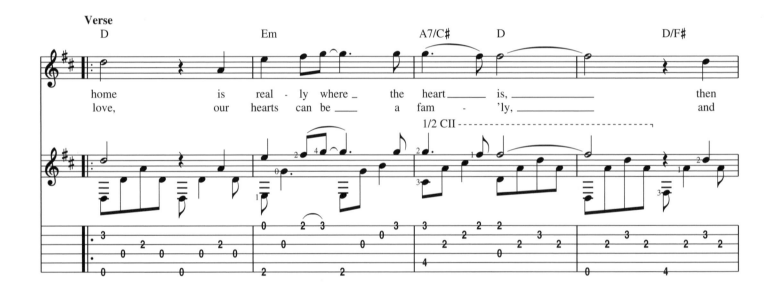

home is real - ly where _ the heart _____ is, _____ then
love, our hearts can be _____ a fam - 'ly, _____ and

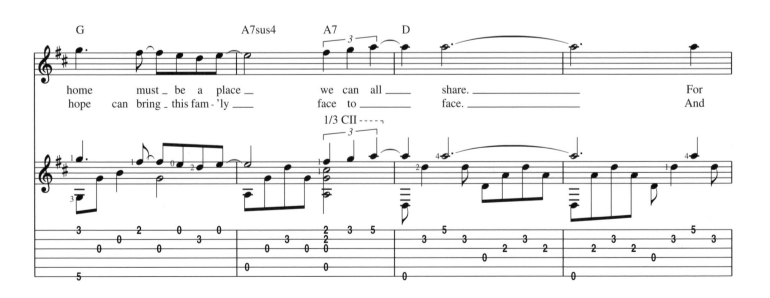

home must _ be a place _ we can all _____ share. _____ For
hope can bring _ this fam - 'ly _____ face to _____ face. _____ And

42

Seekers of Your Heart

Words and Music by Melodie Tunney, Dick Tunney and Beverly Darnall

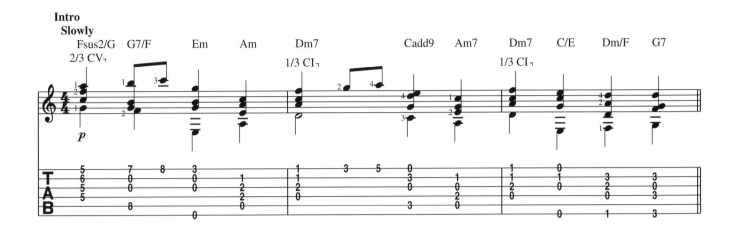

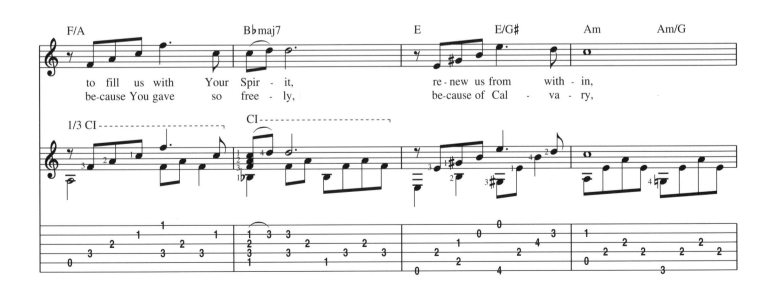

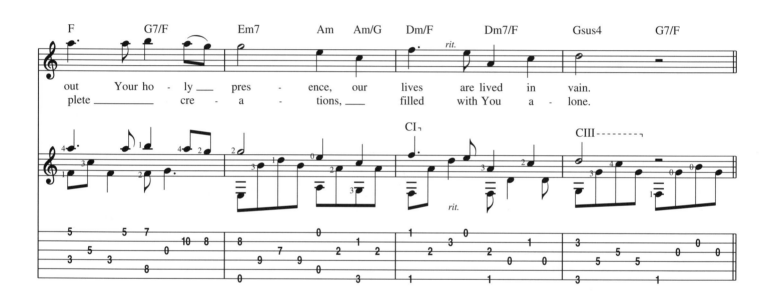

% **Chorus**
A tempo

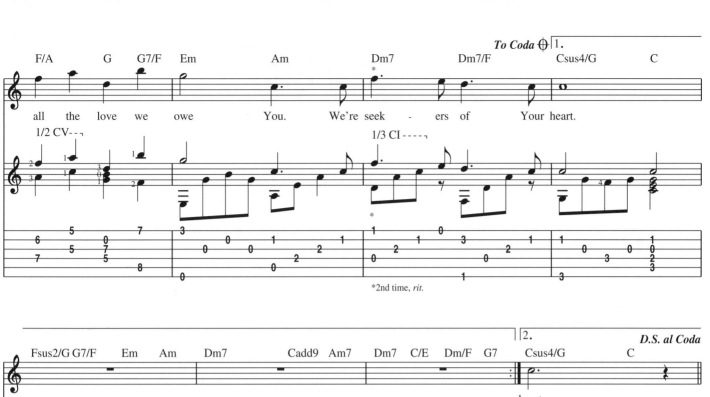

all the love we owe You. We're seek - ers of Your heart.

*2nd time, rit.

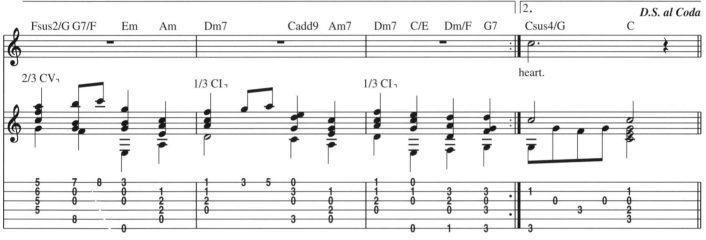

heart.

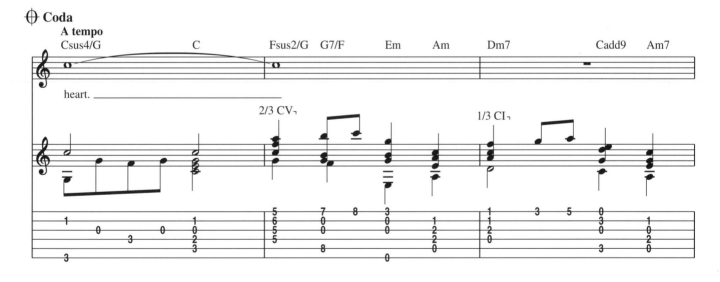

🔴 **Coda**
A tempo

heart.

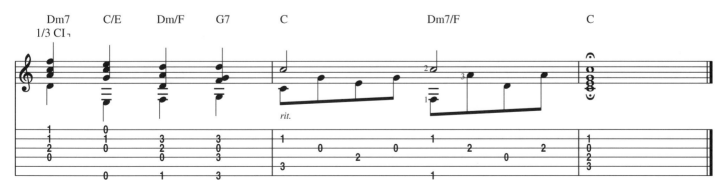

rit.

Parent's Prayer
(Let Go of Two)

Words and Music by Greg Davis

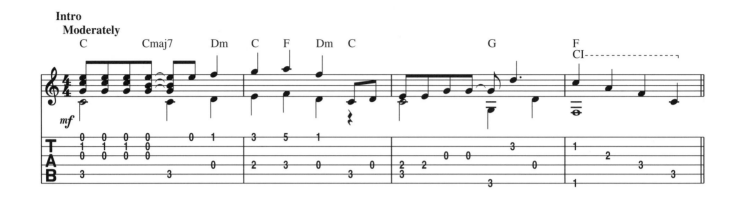

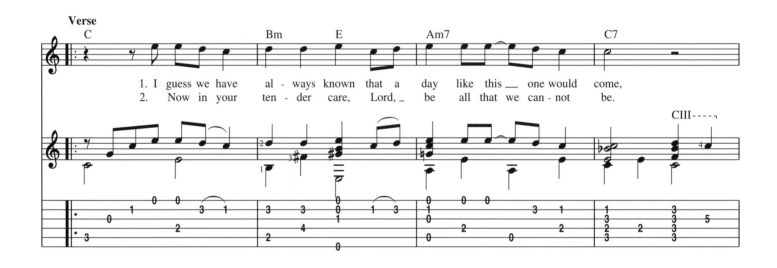

1. I guess we have al-ways known that a day like this __ one would come,
2. Now in your ten-der care, Lord, __ be all that we can-not be.

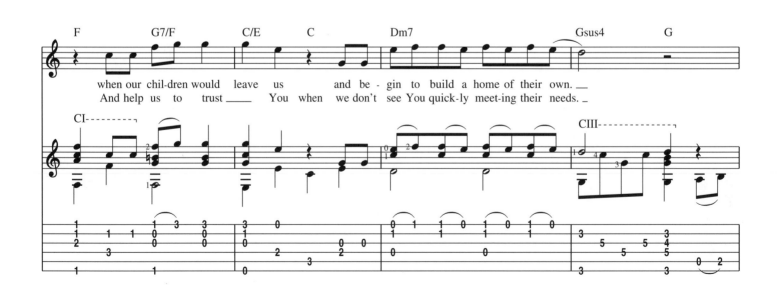

when our chil-dren would leave us and be-gin to build a home of their own. __
And help us to trust ____ You when we don't see You quick-ly meet-ing their needs. _

© 1987 BIRDWING MUSIC
Admin. by EMI CHRISTIAN MUSIC PUBLISHING
All Rights Reserved   Used by Permission

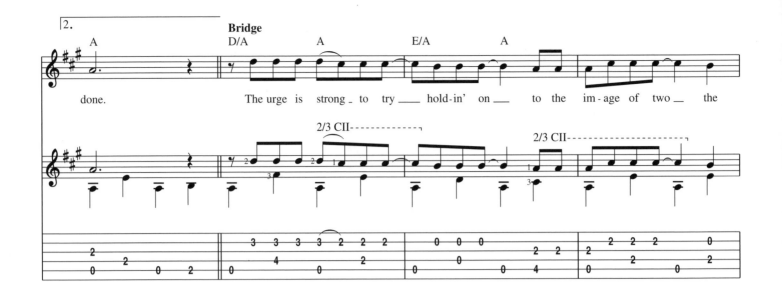

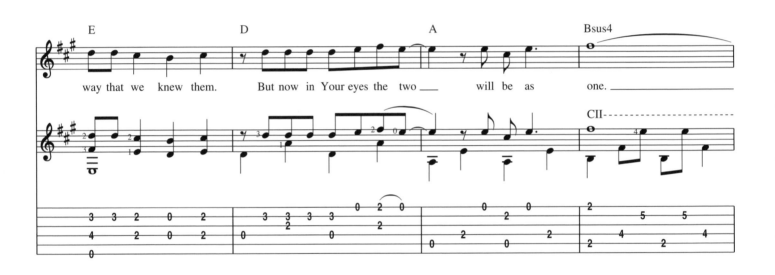

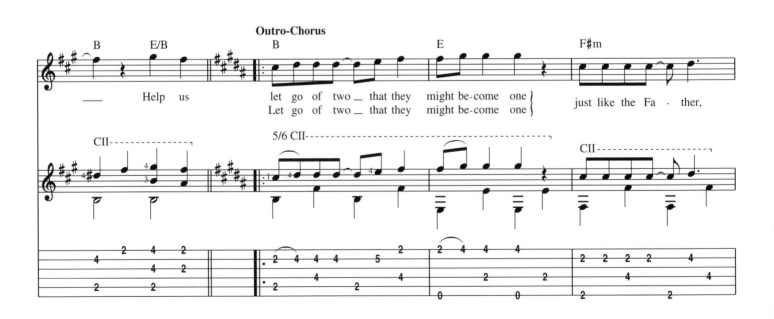

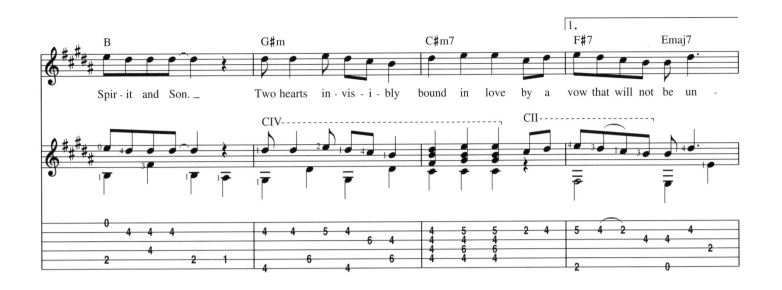

Spir - it and Son. _ Two hearts in - vis - i - bly bound in love by a vow that will not be un -

done. vow that will not be un - done. By a vow that will not be un -

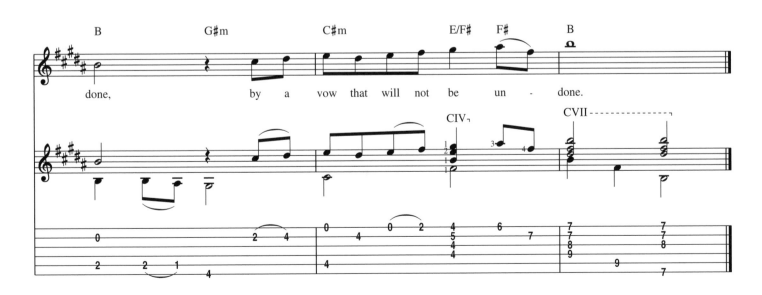

done, by a vow that will not be un - done.

This Is the Day
(A Wedding Song)

Words and Music by Scott Wesley Brown

Outro

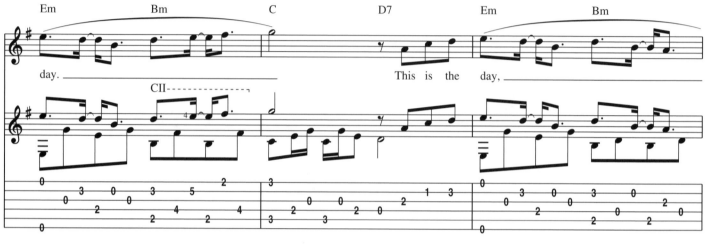

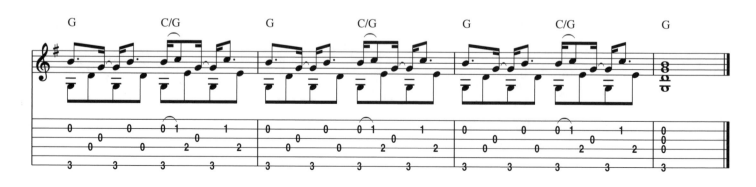

This Very Day

Words and Music by John Elliott and Paul Overstreet

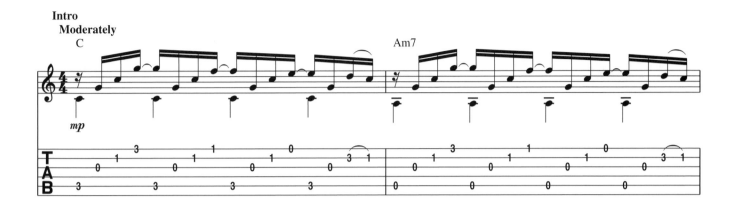

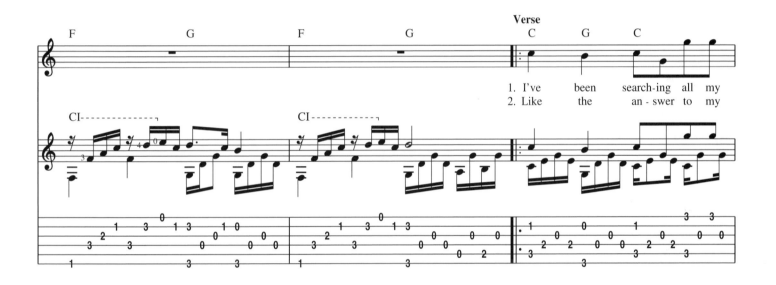

1. I've been search-ing all my
2. Like the an-swer to my

life _____ for the wom-an I was meant to make my wife. And
prayers, _____ from this day on I'll wake to find her there. And

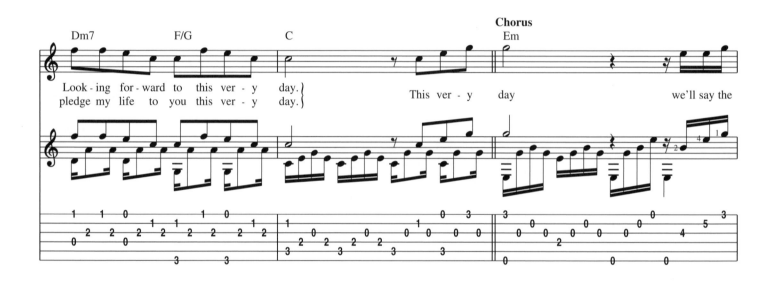

in - to par - a - dise. We're on our way,   and I will face the ris - ing sun   nev - er

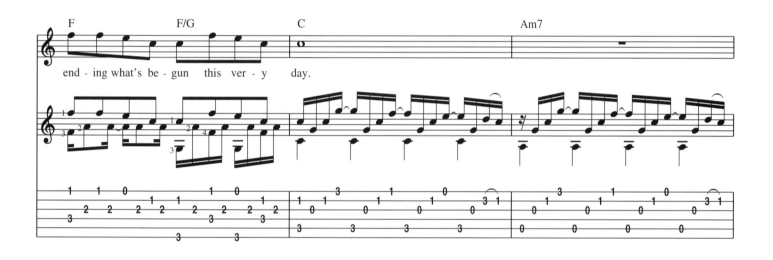

end - ing what's be - gun   this ver - y   day.

Where There Is Love

Words and Music by Phill McHugh and Greg Nelson

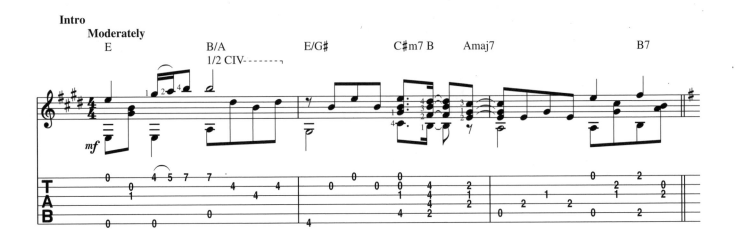

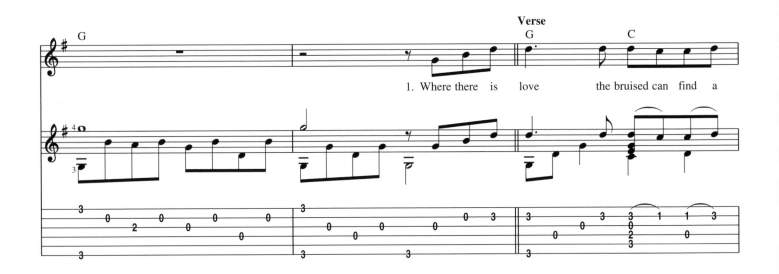

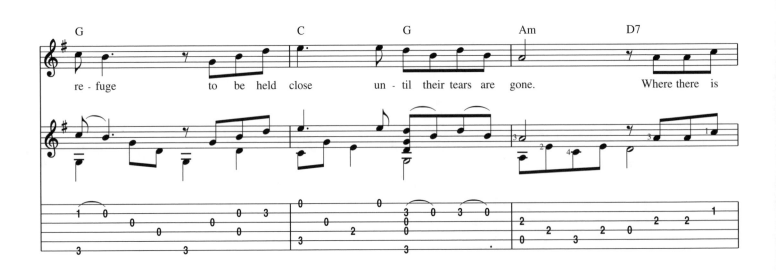

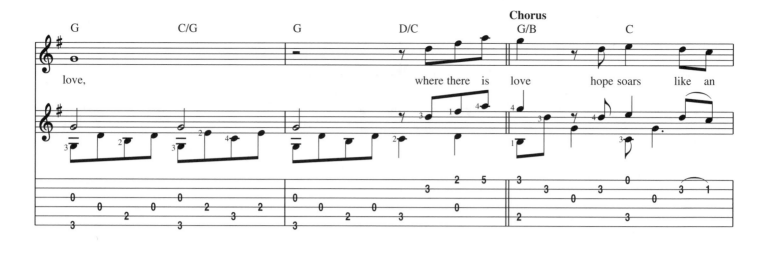

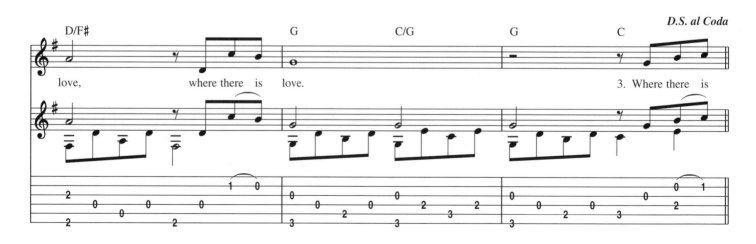

The Wedding

Words and Music by Michael Card

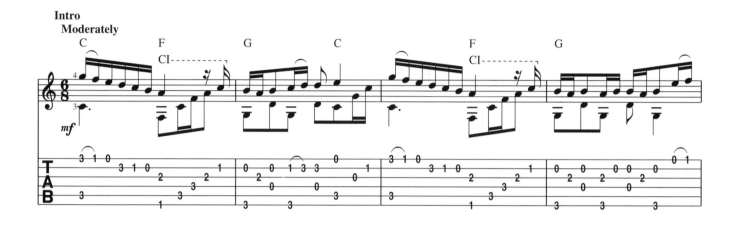

Lord __ of Light, oh come to this wed-ding; take __ the doubt and dark - ness a - way.

Turn ___ the wa - ter of life - less liv - ing to the ___ wine ___ of ___ glad - ness we pray.

Verse

1. Moth - er Mar - y's gen - tly re - quest - ing that
2. So ___ a - midst the laugh - ter and feast - ing,

You ___ might do what - ev - er You can. Though ___ she ___ may ___ be im -
there ___ sits Je - sus full with the fun. He has made ___ them ___ wine be -

pa-tient, she loves You; and so she _ asks _ what she can't un-der-stand. that's yet to come.
cause He is long-ing for a __ wed - ding that's yet to come.

⊕ Coda
Outro

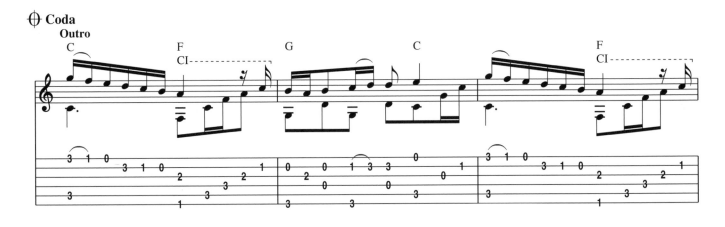

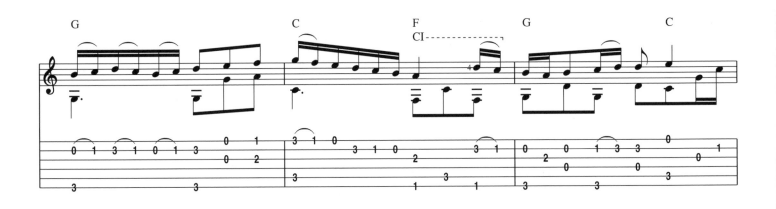

christian**guitar**songbooks

BEST OF AUDIO ADRENALINE

This songbook features note-for-note transcriptions in standard notation & tab for 12 of their top hits: Big House • Can't Take God Away • Chevette • Get Down • Never Gonna Be as Big as Jesus • Walk on Water • more. Includes a band bio and photos.

_____00690418 Guitar Recorded Versions $17.95

BEST OF STEVEN CURTIS CHAPMAN

Features a dozen of his best songs, arranged for fingerstyle guitar: Busy Man • For the Sake of the Call • The Great Adventure • Heaven in the Real World • Hiding Place • His Eyes • His Strength Is Perfect • Hold On to Jesus • I Will Be Here • More to This Life • My Turn Now • What Would I Say.

_____00699138 Fingerstyle Guitar $10.95

BEST OF STEVEN CURTIS CHAPMAN FOR EASY GUITAR

15 songs including: The Great Adventure • Heaven in the Real World • His Strength Is Perfect • I Will Be There • More to This Life.

_____00702033 Easy Guitar with Notes & Tab $12.95

STEVEN CURTIS CHAPMAN GUITAR COLLECTION

12 of his most popular songs transcribed note-for-note for guitar, including: Fort the Sake of the Call • The Great Adventure • Heaven in the Real World • His Eyes • I Will Be Here • Lord of the Dance • More to This Life • Signs of Life • and more.

_____00690293 Guitar Recorded Versions $19.95

CONTEMPORARY CHRISTIAN FAVORITES

20 great easy guitar arrangements of contemporary Christian songs, including: El Shaddai • Friends • He Is Able • I Will Be Here • In the Name of the Lord • In Christ Alone • Love in Any Language • Open My Heart • Say the Name • Thy Word • Via Dolorosa • and more.

_____00702006 E-Z Guitar With Tab $10.95

CONTEMPORARY CHRISTIAN FAVORITES

17 great songs arranged for fingerstyle guitar: Butterfly Kisses • Chain of Grace • El Shaddai • Friend of a Wounded Heart • Friends • He Is Able • His Strength Is Perfect • Love in Any Language • Open My Heart • Say the Name • Thy Word • Via Dolorosa • more.

_____00699137 Fingerstyle Guitar $10.95

DC TALK – JESUS FREAK

Matching folio with note-for-note transcriptions to this contemporary Christian band's cross-over album. Songs include: Between You and Me • Jesus Freak • In the Light • Colored People • and more. Also includes photos.

_____00690184 Guitar Recorded Versions $19.95

DC TALK – SUPERNATURAL

Includes transcriptions in notes & tab of the 13 songs from Supernatural: Consume Me • Dive • Fearless • Godsend • Into Jesus • It's Killing Me • My Friend (So Long) • Red Letters • Since I Met You • Supernatural • There Is a Treason at Sea • The Truth • Wanna Be Loved.

_____00690333 Guitar Recorded Versions $19.95

DELIRIOUS? – MEZZAMORPHIS

14 songs in notes & tab from the third album by this Christian punk/pop band from England: Beautiful Sun • Blindfold • Bliss • Deeper 99 • Follow • Gravity • Heaven • It's OK • Jesus' Blood • Kiss Your Feet • Love Falls Down • Metamorphis • The Mezzanine Floor • See the Star. Includes photos.

_____00690378 Guitar Recorded Versions $19.95

FAVORITE HYMNS FOR EASY GUITAR

48 hymns, including: All Hail the Power of Jesus' Name • Amazing Grace • Be Thou My Vision • Blessed Assurance • Fairest Lord Jesus • I Love to Tell the Story • In the Garden • Let Us Break Bread Together • Rock of Ages • Were You There? • When I Survey the Wondrous Cross • and more.

_____00702041 E-Z Guitar with Notes & Tab $9.95

GLORIOUS HYMNS

Large, easy-to-read notation and tablature for 30 inspirational hymns: Abide with Me • Amazing Grace • Blessed Assurance • Come Christians Join to Sing • In the Garden • Jacob's Ladder • Rock of Ages • What a Friend We Have in Jesus • Wondrous Love • more.

_____00699192 EZ Play Guitar $7.95

GOSPEL FAVORITES FOR GUITAR

An amazing collection of 50 favorites, including: Amazing Grace • Did You Stop to Pray This Morning • He Lives • His Name Is Wonderful • How Great Thou Art • The King Is Coming • My God Is Real • Nearer, My God, To Thee • The Old Rugged Cross • Take My Hand, Precious Lord • Turn Your Radio On • Will the Circle Be Unbroken • and more.

_____00699374 EZ Guitar with Notes & Tab $14.95

BEST OF AMY GRANT

118 of her best arranged for easy guitar, including; Angels • Baby Baby • Big Yellow Taxi • Doubly Good to You • El Shaddai • Every Heartbeat • Find a Way • Good for Me • House of Love • Lead Me On • Lucky One • Tennessee Christmas • and more.

_____00702099 Easy Guitar with Notes & Tab $9.95

GREATEST HYMNS FOR GUITAR

48 hymns, including: Abide with Me • Amazing Grace • Be Still My Soul • Glory to His Name • In the Garden • and more.

_____00702116 Easy Guitar with Notes & Tab $7.95

MAKING SOME NOISE
–TODAY'S MODERN CHRISTIAN ROCK

13 transcriptions, including: Big House • Cup • Flood • God • Jesus Freak • Shine • Soulbait • and more.

_____00690216 Guitar Recorded Versions $14.95

MXPX – THE EVER PASSING MOMENT

This matching folio to the release by this punk/pop Christian band includes note-for-note transcriptions for 15 tracks: Buildings Tumble • Educated Guess • Foolish • Here with Me • Is the Answer in the Question? • It's Undeniable • Misplaced Memories • My Life Story • The Next Big Thing • and more. Includes cool photos and tab.

_____00690448 Guitar Recorded Versions $19.95

THE BEST OF NEWSBOYS

13 songs in notes & TAB from these popular Christian rockers: Breakfast • Breathe • Dear Shame • Entertaining Angels • God Is Not a Secret • I Cannot Get You Out of My System • Real Good Thing • Shine • Spirit Thing • Step up to the Microphone • Strong Love • Take Me to Your Leader • Woo Hoo.

_____00690345 Guitar Recorded Versions $17.95

P.O.D. – THE FUNDAMENTAL ELEMENTS OF SOUTHTOWN

Matching folio with 16 songs, including: Bullet the Blue Sky • Follow Me • Freestyle • Image • Lie Down • Outkast • Rock the Party (Off the Hook) • Shouts • Southtown • and more.

_____00690456 Guitar Recorded Versions..........................$19.95

PRAISE AND WORSHIP FOR GUITAR

25 easy arrangements, including: As the Deer • Glorify Thy Name • He Is Exalted • Holy Ground • How Excellent Is Thy Name • Majesty • Thou Art Worthy • You Are My Hiding Place • more.

_____00702125 Easy Guitar with Notes & Tab $8.95

SONICFLOOD

6 songs transcribed note-for-note, including: Carried Away • Holy One • I Could Sing of Your Love Forever • I Need You • My Refuge • There's Something About That Name.

_____00690385 Guitar Recorded Versions $19.95

TODAY'S CHRISTIAN FAVORITES

19 songs, including: Daystar • Find Us Faithful • Go West Young Man • God and God Alone • He Is Exalted • I Will Choose Christ • Jubilate • My Turn Now • A Perfect Heart • Revive Us, O Lord • and more.

_____00702042 Easy Guitar with Notes & Tab $8.95

TODAY'S CHRISTIAN ROCK FOR EASY GUITAR

Over 10 powerful contemporary Christian songs. Includes: Between You and Me (dc Talk) • Flood (Jars of Clay) • Kiss Me (Sixpence None the Richer) • Lord of the Dance (Steven Curtis Chapman) • On My Knees (Jaci Velasquez) • and more.

_____00702124 Easy Guitar with Notes & Tab $8.95

Prices and availability subject to change without notice.

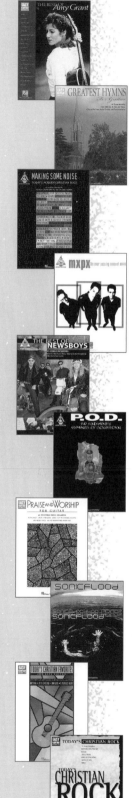

FOR MORE INFORMATION, SEE YOUR LOCAL MUSIC DEALER, OR WRITE TO:

 **HAL·LEONARD®** CORPORATION

7777 W. BLUEMOUND RD. P.O. BOX 13819 MILWAUKEE, WI 53213

www.halleonard.com

ALL BOOKS INCLUDE NOTES & TABLATURE